WOMAN AT MID-LIFE
Moving Beyond Stereotypes

Vernie Dale

LIGUORI
PUBLICATIONS

One Liguori Drive
Liguori, Missouri 63057
(314) 464-2500

Imprimi Potest:
John F. Dowd, C.SS.R.
Provincial, St. Louis Province
Redemptorist Fathers

Imprimatur:
+ Edward J. O'Donnell
Vicar General, Archdiocese of St. Louis

ISBN 0-89243-230-6
Library of Congress Catalog Card Number: 84-52884

Cover photo by H. Armstrong Roberts

Table of Contents

Caught in a Storm

Something began looming on the sunny horizon of Ann's life just before her youngest child started school. An attractive and responsible mother of three, Ann had been very active for many years in parish work, had made a Marriage Encounter with her husband, and had no financial or marital problems. She planned to go back to school to update her college degree, and then get a job. But all that was forgotten as a stifling sense of depression closed over her that summer. Within the next three months, Ann attempted suicide twice and finally entered a mental institution. She was only thirty-nine years old.

Even though he died over six hundred years before Ann was born, the great poet Dante would have understood her experience. He began his *Divine Comedy* with a description of a life-event which occurred when he was almost her age: "Midway in my life's journey, I woke to find myself alone in a dark wood. Its very memory gives a shape to fear." In 1554, when Teresa of Avila also was thirty-nine, she wrote of a profoundly unsettling time, a period of vague dissatisfaction with her life, culminating in an experience when "it seemed to me my heart broke." Centuries later, in 1914, the great psychologist Carl Jung withdrew from his post at the University of Zurich and entered a long period of darkness and inner turmoil. He, too, was thirty-nine.

Something happens to men and women just as they approach the zenith of their lives. It seems to come as suddenly as a violent storm; and, like tornado victims who can only stare at the ruins of their homes, many husbands and wives in their late thirties and early forties find themselves in the midst of emotional or marital wreckage.

Since this crisis of mid-life approaches sooner for most women than for most men, it is usually the wife who first senses something is coming, that something is wrong; and unless she knows what is happening to her and how to handle it, she may eventually be driven to the brink of depression or divorce.

Being a good Christian does not spare one from this passage. Psychologists tell us it is one of the experiences, like adolescence, through which all of us must pass if we are to achieve full maturity. In fact, it may be Christian women who are the hardest hit. We have learned so many "shoulds": we should feel fulfilled if we are doing God's will; we should be grateful for our middle-class blessings; we should feel love for children and spouse.

In this age of women's liberation, if we do not feel as free as society says we are, we may begin to question our commitments. When others are escaping marriages they view as the source of all the hurt, we may begin to lose faith in marriage itself, lose faith in a lasting as well as personally fulfilling relationship with a spouse. We not only have to cope with the pressures of society but also with the pressure of our religion, and we may feel trapped between the passion of emotions deep within us and the Christian ideal of patience with others and trust in God.

"My Marriage Is Not Enough"

We feel it coming, something in the air when we get up day after day, a far-off dark thing just outside our awareness. We don't want to look at it, and try concentrating on other things; but it always comes closer, like an approaching storm. Then one day, like Ann, we find ourselves overwhelmed by emotion, and our own tears force us to admit our deep unhappiness, our terrible frustration.

Our logic berates us: "You have everything you could possibly want — a hardworking husband, growing children, your religion, your home, a car, TV. What *more* do you want?" We don't know; we have no answer for our logical selves. But, instinctively, we know we are surging with life, with a passionate longing and desire for something. We know we have a lot to give, way down deep; and we yearn to pour it out in some way, somehow, on someone. "I am split in two!" Ann cried out to her counselor. "A part of me wants to feel loving, wants to cherish Bill and the kids and find fulfillment in what I do for them, but it's not enough. Oh, God, I was born to do something great, something meaningful, but there's nothing but this emptiness all around!"

Over and over, women ask themselves questions which bring great pain, questions like: "Is this all there is? Is this all I'm fit for?" These questions are painful because there seem to be no answers; we ourselves do not know what we want. We only know that the realization gradually comes upon us that husband, home, and children are not enough anymore.

We become bitterly resentful of the meaninglessness of our tasks. Keeping track of the children's schedules, doing the family budget, making dinner and beds day after day — all a jumble of detail, not worth doing. Forty years have already passed for us, and the next forty seem only like the long slide toward old age and death.

Yet, it is also a time in our lives that often feels a lot like adolescence. We are in almost constant emotional turmoil, for our own deeply felt potential seeks desperately to be set free. There is something more to us, more to life; yet something is also being stifled and blocked. The only thing we know how to do, the only way we know to get some control over what we feel, is to find someone to blame.

The closest one is our husband. He never seems to notice our pain, or else reacts with exasperation. "Why don't you get out more," Ann's husband told her, "now that the kids are all in school. Take a class or join a group, for Pete's sake. You certainly have the time for it." Or else he becomes angry, and gives a message something like this: "I worked hard to give you this house, this life. I'm still working hard, and stuck in this dead-end job. The least you can do is be happy with what you have."

His lack of understanding hurts, hurts a lot, because he is saying exactly what our logic has already told us many times. One part of us asks, "Why can't I be content?" But the other half cries out, "I need something *more*!"

Perhaps our spouse reads his paper, goes to bed as usual, and inside we want to scream at him, "Why are you so dead? Don't you *see* me?" We feel that we are dying, that our life together is dying; and no one seems able to stop it. Were we ever in love at all? Is there anything left anymore?

To find out, we would have to talk to one another, make some attempt to communicate the pain. But every time we try, out of our deep hurt burst angry words of blame. When it is too late, and he has left the room, we may bitterly regret what we have said. Yet, way down deep it is how we *feel,* and nothing on earth can change that.

After a while the hurt becomes too great for us even to try to express it. We have no words for what is wrong, except angry ones. Our husband says we have become impossible to please, impossible to live with. He just opts out, spending more and more time away from the house. Looming before us is the terrible suspicion that the only solution is divorce, to bury a marriage that died long ago.

Lonely Suffering

Women tend to be especially sensitive to emotional suffering and highly dependent on others for self-esteem. Thus they find the turmoil of mid-life devastating. Because it generally happens to them first, women experience a great deal of profound loneliness. Children are busy with school and friends; and husband is usually at the height of his career, ignoring pretty successfully his own inner discontent. Whether she works outside the home or not, household chores, viewed by society as trivial and beneath an intelligent person, are usually her responsibility. Her *husband's* work is undoubtedly meaningful because the money he earns supports the whole family. *Her* work, whether in the home or at a low-paying job, is becoming increasingly meaningless. Yet, if a wife resents the attention her husband focuses on his job, she winds up besieged by guilt: could *she* go out and get a job that would support the entire family? She knows, in the vast majority of cases, the answer is no, even if she could summon up the courage to try.

In mid-life a woman's self-esteem is almost nonexistent. She wants to continue to believe in the passionate potential she feels deep within her; yet, she is becoming anxious that her dreams have already been betrayed, and is beginning to fear that it may all somehow be her own fault. The children she has spent her whole life caring for do not need her so much anymore, and may not be turning out to be the persons she had hoped they would be. The husband she gave up everything for seems to have priorities above her. She is angry at them all, angry at herself, and terribly ashamed because she feels such unchristian hatred and selfish bitterness.

Interlaced with all this anger, then, is overwhelming guilt, the guilt her Christianity brings her. Isn't giving yourself in a life of service the most important thing there is? Aren't Christian husbands and wives called to fulfillment in marital relationships? And what am I doing to the children? As guilt builds, so does self-doubt. "Why am I the only one who sees a problem?" wonders the wife. She begins to doubt her own perceptions, her own intuition, because most of the time her husband professes to see no difficulties whatsoever.

The problem is further complicated for a woman in the crisis of mid-life because she is extremely reluctant to seek professional help. It is very expensive, and she is convinced that she is not worth it, particularly at a time when the family is already reeling under college tuition costs, higher car insurance for teen drivers, braces for preadolescents, and those puzzling increases in her own doctor bills. Her own husband tells her there is really nothing wrong: she is just bored and "looking for something to worry about." She deeply resents this; yet he is, after all, the one who has to pay the bill.

If the husband regards counseling as an expensive luxury for his wife and repeatedly asserts that no real problems exist, then it is easy for a wife of low self-esteem to cop out and agree. She is already guilty at feeling so angry, and may see nothing in her outward life to warrant such turmoil. There may be no overt marital or family problems beyond those others tell her that she herself is precipitating. And if there *are* other troubles — a teen on drugs or a husband chasing his fading youth in the form of his secretary — then *these* are regarded as the problem. Having a mid-life crisis sounds laughable, a luxury indeed, compared to these "real" troubles.

Women at mid-life, then, usually bear a great burden of suffering, and they generally bear it alone. They are very ashamed of the emotions they feel and try to hide them beneath a veneer of brave coping. They desperately need someone to help; but, by and large, not even their church notices — even though this crisis is now known to be a time when profound spiritual conversion is truly possible.

This loneliness makes the anger, frustration, and profound self-doubt of mid-life a terribly painful burden, so painful that the human psyche would do anything to get rid of it. When we can no longer bear such a heavy and hurting weight, we instinctively try to get it off us, fling it away from us, rejecting the pain with all our energy. In other words, we "project" the blame onto someone else.

This is fatally easy to do, especially for married couples, for who of us is without fault? Who of us has no weakness that our spouses can find it easier and less painful to attack than her or his own? Projection is at work when a wife who denies her own inner anger focuses on the testiness of her husband, or when a husband who is afraid of his own emotions becomes exasperated with his wife's.

Such acute discontent with one's marriage often leads at last to an all-pervading discontent with oneself. The pressure of the terrible need that is not being fulfilled outside ourselves finally forces us to look within.

"I Am Not Enough"

We know something is crumbling, breaking up, dissolving because we can feel the pain of it. First we think it is our marriage, then we think it is happening to us ourselves. For days on end we function with no purpose, performing meaningless tasks or else finding them too complicated even to attempt. We no longer feel resentment, only despair, and act at times like a wound-up robot going through the motions. "I knew I was alive somewhere deep down," Ann said, "only because I could feel tears running down my face. I was crying too much to be dead."

The days seem to converge into one great hurt. Everything our spouse says, or doesn't say, belittles us. We look into the mirror and see a gray-faced woman fading away into nothingness. We feel we have wasted our whole life, and it is too late to do anything about it. No effort of determined willpower, no shopping spree or eating binge, seems able to fill the aching emptiness or to stop the hurt.

Housewives may see other women finding jobs, updating degrees, involved in doing good for others, coping just fine. Why can't we follow suit? One woman discovered how terrified she was of going back to school. "What if all those years of changing diapers have calcified my brain?" she worried. "What if I'm not as smart or as capable as I think I am?" Whether they work outside the home or not, women fear their own ambition, fear the humiliation of yet another failure, and so hesitate to try. We remain helpless in the grip of our fear and doubt, thinking, "What can I really do to make a contribution?" We realize how dependent we have become, in what an ivory tower we've lived. Yet, how we long to be free!

We look to our spouse to give us permission, to do it for us, to give us courage and a reason to live. But his brooding silence berates us: "Stand on your own two feet, can't you? I have my own problems. I, too, see that there's nowhere to go but down. I, too, feel I have wasted my life in this job. Grow up and leave me alone!"

His unspoken words add to our own deep bitterness, our sense of inadequacy and guilt. We tell ourselves we *can't* become independent, *can't* become whoever we were meant to be. Society or men or our children or our religion or our lack of education or our lack of assertiveness won't let us. We do not know who we really are or what we want, and haven't the foggiest notion of how to free the potential within us.

Perhaps the lowest rung is reached when we become aware of our own deep-lying hate. We look at our spouse and see our own deadness, our own weakness, and we hate him. We look at our children, as Ann did, and see only selfish creatures that demand and demand and give nothing back. But most of all, we despise ourselves. No Christian woman, no human being, should hate so much. No twentieth-century woman should feel so dependent and inadequate, so trapped as we. Our own terrible unhappiness makes no sense, and we fear we must be going crazy. Instinctively, we know that blaming others can lead to divorce; yet, blaming ourselves can lead to depression or even suicide.

For the first time in our lives we have been forced to look within, and we confront a side of ourselves that we hate — a shrill, tearful, and vastly inadequate human being. I am not enough, not even for myself.

1

Dangerous Escape Routes

In mid-life, then, men and women often feel that a storm of terrible force is enveloping them, a whirling darkness that will pull everything down around them and leave them with nothing. They glimpse a vortex of emptiness and, in panic, try to flee. Many people in mid-life do not realize that the vortex is really a path to greater maturity and must be entered into. Instead, they turn away. They seek to escape, and this becomes actually more dangerous than weathering the storm itself.

This escape can take either of two routes, and fleeing along either one of them is the way of regression, the way of slow psychological and spiritual death.

Immature "Masculine" Reactions

One "way out" lies in **using one's intellect or senses to deny the emptiness.** Psychologists have long associated a high development of the analytical powers of the intellect and the data-collecting powers of the five senses with the masculine role and its outer-orientation, just as they have linked a high development of the emotions and intuition to the wifely and motherly roles and their inner orientation. In the past, it was most often the husband who reacted to the mid-life crisis in the immature "masculine" way. But, as women are becoming more and more free to use their own gifts of logic and objective analysis, they, too, are becoming more and more capable of *misusing* them in a way that avoids rather than confronts the challenge to change.

When facing feelings she can't understand or a vision of herself she can't accept, a modern woman is free, just like her husband always has been, to deny that problems surfacing through her intuitive perception of the situation exist at all. "I'm too strong, too smart, too 'with it' to have a crisis," she tells herself. This is a very attractive *idea:* the mid-life crisis happens only to unintelligent and somewhat old-fashioned housewives, bored and foolish women who never take life by the horns and wrestle it to do their will. The "I'm too smart" *idea* appeals to modern women, just as it always has to men, because its *logic* soothes us with fantasies of our own power and invulnerability, tells us we are in control of everything, even our own growth. But the fact is that mid-life is a stage of development in the life of every human person. Whether we are housewives or career professionals, an opportunity for further maturing and a chance to become even more whole will be given to each of us. Turning away from this chance by convincing ourselves that it can't happen to us is refusing the challenge.

Another way of avoiding a heightened awareness of our own vulnerability is an offshoot of the first: **ignoring**

our sensitive inner emotional bonds to others in an assertion of our own independence and toughness. This is often done with a great show of competence or busyness that says, "See how important and needed I am!" Husbands have long been guilty of throwing themselves into their work to avoid growing in relational ways; but wives, too, can become overextended — with housework, a job, volunteerism, or planning everyone's day. Ann, for example, was spending hours deciding on activities for her three children, arranging their leisure time schedules, driving them to scouts, soccer, baseball, music lessons, and nature programs. She would remind them constantly about what had to be done when, what outfits were suitable to wear, and took responsibility for getting them everywhere on time. Her mind was full of a swarm of buzzing details, of activities she initiated because she thought she had to. The result? She began to resent her own children; and she never had time to face her own emptiness, her own needs, until it was almost too late.

This kind of escapism often hides behind a veneer of belligerent independence, vocalized by some feminists who assert, "Women don't need men, children, or *anyone* to be fulfilled." The power of this statement lies in its partial truth — for too long many women allowed their individual personality to remain merged with a mother, a husband, or a daughter in ways which were psychologically stunting. For too long women believed they were powerless without men, and relied on others to give their lives meaning. We now realize that no woman needs one particular person for her survival as a human being, but we all need *someone,* some other who cares. Even staunch feminists know they need a sisterhood. This is true because — as we see so clearly in families —

we are interconnected through a hundred invisible yet very strong bonds. *Independence,* then, must eventually give way to *interdependence,* for this is the wisdom of humility and part of the process of truly growing up.

In her instinctive search for this kind of maturity, a woman in mid-life may decide to work for pay outside the home. A job, she hopes, will give her the independence she longs for and add meaning to a life that has become increasingly boring and empty. But the most important reason for acquiring a job is the paycheck, because that represents the affirmation for which she is so starved. Unlike her job at home, a paying job clearly states that a woman is a person whose time is valuable and who has the power our society most respects — the power to spend money.

These are very strong reasons for seeking employment, but it is important that a wife at this time of life look very carefully at them lest getting a job become just another way to escape her emerging self. More and more women are asking themselves if going back to work because of "financial need" isn't merely a way to fund a life-style that focuses on *wants* and not on Christian stewardship and simplicity. Others are asking if the desirability and "meaning" of a particular job lie in the joy and challenge of the work or only in the money it pays. Others see that jobs that truly help others in need are being passed over solely because they are unpaid.

There is also a danger for the woman who has held a job right along to contribute to the family's income. The mid-life crisis comes for her, too, and makes the same demands for reassessment of life-style. Tired after a long day at work and faced with household chores as well, it is easy for the working woman to avoid such questions as: How can I develop my talents further? How can I make what I do a freer choice? How can I have more time and energy for the people I love?

Working outside the home or not, competing successfully with men or not, our "job" as Christian women is to make visible to the world our deepest goodness, our joy, and our compassion. Our "job" is to change the world — step by step, bit by bit — by freeing our inner radiance to grow and shine upon our immediate environment. It does not really matter what work we do, as long as it is not done to escape becoming our true selves.

In the long run, women must remember that meaning and affirmation do not come from without. These are gifts only we can give ourselves. And this is what the mid-life crisis is all about — gifting ourselves, accepting God's gift of our entire selves, and thus becoming whole. This can be done from a wheelchair or from a judge's bench, from a grocery check-out line or from a cloister, from a space shuttle or from a kitchen.

A third way to escape the mid-life challenge involves **focusing on others instead of on oneself.** This, too, can be subtly aggressive because, instead of developing her own powers of logic and observation to discover what is happening within, a wife may use these as a weapon against others. She may magnify faults, criticize everything, nitpick. There is, of course, no question that other people have imperfections, but if these become a woman's chief focus she can find herself becoming the classic nag. Part of this reaction may involve singling out and seizing upon one person — boss, husband, teenage child, or elderly parent — as *the* source of all her upset. There may indeed be a great deal of tension in these relationships, but one person is seldom the only cause. Everyone caught in a painful situation has contributed to it in some way, and all can benefit from a deeper understanding of the dynamic reciprocity involved when people are close. The worst aspect of this kind of projection is the hurt it brings, not so much to others but to the woman herself. Her own inner woundedness is never looked at, never seen, and, therefore, never healed.

In mid-life a woman's first duty is to develop, by using them, her powers of objective observation to look inside herself, weighing very carefully her judgment of others. Her energy cannot be wasted in aggression when she will need it to journey within.

Some women waste their energy in a different way, by spending large amounts of it trying to prove how capable they are or how much they are doing for others. Because this kind of woman is often very successful in a pastoral or professional career, the only one not convinced is often she herself. Such women sometimes fall into the trap of hiding behind their own competence or behind a veneer of concern for people, and avoid looking at their own longings and limitations.

"Thinking" as used by Carl Jung does not mean intelligence or capability or professional success. It means looking at my undefended self, assessing my strong and weak points as well as my deepest *needs.* Just as an actor's ability to emote "feelings" is no guarantee of his true sensitivity to himself or others, so also the professional's competence is no guarantee that she uses the objectivity toward herself that is needed for inner wholeness.

A final escape route or immature reaction to the mid-life experience is a **surrender to hedonism,** to using our senses of touching, tasting, seeing, or hearing to turn off our awareness of our own inner emptiness. Drugs or alcohol used to be the "masculine" way to escape, but these now present more and more problems to women.

Extramarital affairs become very real possibilities at mid-life because women long for tenderness and affirmation; they feel deep within a passionate desire to pour out their very selves. Often, they feel unappreciated and taken for granted by their families; and they are very vulnerable to someone who really *sees* them at last.

Buying binges are a subtle form of this hedonistic way to "escape" mid-life bleakness. Janice, for example, used shopping at the local mall as her only entertainment, one which made her feel useful to her family. Wasn't she "providing" for them? Couldn't the kids "always use" one more school outfit? But, gradually, Janice became aware of the fact that she was a person in her own right, with talents of her own, with responsibilities to her world. Shopping was not so important anymore. Eventually, Janice went through all her closets, discarding literally dozens of once-worn blouses and unneeded slacks her children had never even tried on. When she was done she had three large bags of clothing which she gave to a needy neighbor. "I was always trying to fill up my life's basic emptiness in the only way I knew how," she said. "Buying all that stuff for my kids meant I was a good mother. Buying outfits for myself meant I valued myself and wanted to look good. But way down deep I knew it was a lie. Way down deep I knew I was impoverished as a person and needed to grow."

* * * * *

Denying a crisis exists, pseudoindependence, projecting the problem onto others, overconsumption — all these are ways to use our intellect and our senses to avoid looking within. They are all based on the fear that who I am is too terrible a person to live with, that my emptiness can never be filled, that somewhere deep inside me is a black hole that will devour everything I am. Yet, like a pregnancy, the mid-life passage will not "just go away" by my refusing to deal with it.

Immature "Feminine" Reactions

Very different kinds of escape routes have long been associated with the highly developed "feminine" or inner-oriented powers of emotion and intuition. Just as logic and physical sensation can be used to avoid coming to terms with oneself, so can a person's emotions and intuitive power.

This can happen in a variety of ways. If one of the outgoing ways to escape change was overinvolvement in the practical affairs of daily living, its inner-oriented counterpart is **overinvolvement in a world of fantasy.** This world is conveniently at hand, a multimillion dollar business in our society. We can cry over the plight of the soap-opera heroine, spending hours living a fictitious life. We can make love over and over to the dark and dangerous stranger of paperback romances, overcoming all kinds of obstacles to "true love." We can focus our entire attention on the movie stars or royalty, portrayed in drugstore tabloids, or minutely examine the motives of people we barely know in coffee-klatch gossiping. This is not to say, of course, that watching TV or reading or socializing with the neighbors is wrong; but substituting these for confronting ourselves and dealing with our own emptiness is just another evasion of the challenge mid-life brings.

Another inner-oriented escape route bears telltale resemblance to the aggressive kind of independence we looked at earlier. In that former case, women told themselves they needed no one; in this case it's a matter of **believing that everything depends on us alone.** Many of us who are wives and mothers have been brought up to believe we are responsible for many things. We think we must keep peace in the home at any cost, must settle the children's every quarrel, must avoid getting our husbands angry by telling them how we feel, must smooth over any differences before they erupt into open confrontation. "Don't bother Daddy when he's reading the paper," we say anxiously, instead of letting Daddy speak for himself. We *hover,* trying to keep everyone cheerful, cringing at any hint of a raised voice. We have taken it upon ourselves to fit our children into a noise-free environment for our spouses while seeking to assure the painless, conflictless, emotional development of the children as well. Being a "good mother" or a "supportive wife" has somehow come to mean molding the personalities of family members to fit into our idea of how things should be: bright, pleasant, and always cheerful.

It is extremely hard for such tense and fearful persons to grow up. Maturity always involves expressing our needs, confronting others with ourselves as we are, and trusting in the goodness and instinct toward growth present in our own spouse and children. Our intuition tells us we are *responsible,* and this is true, but not for everyone and for everything. We must always bear in mind and heart that others have responsibility for their own lives, and let them shoulder it.

We can **misuse our intuition** about things in another way, **and tell ourselves that we can do nothing about our own situation and our own weaknesses.** When we first look within and see the terrible *need* there, our first reaction, as we have seen, could be to deny the reality of our own incompleteness: "I'm *not* that kind of person! I'm too strong to be so wounded!" But others may react in an opposite extreme and tell themselves a different lie: "I'm too weak to handle this. There's no way out for me." These women stumble into the painful spiral of their own emotions and fall into the very trap they sense is closing in on their lives. They see themselves as victims of society and blame their own lack of education or experience on sexual discrimination, their perception that "no one pays attention to me because I'm a woman."

A woman can shift attention away from inner need by constantly seeing her "rights" being trampled upon. There is absolutely no doubt that women are discriminated against, and often in very pervasive and subtle ways; but a defensive person chooses to see an insult instead of her own problem. One woman, chronically late to work and a constant complainer, often resorted to tears when her boss asked her about unfinished work. At last the company was forced to let her go, whereupon the woman immediately charged discrimination. Instead of taking seriously the suggestions of others, instead of facing her own very real problems squarely, a woman may choose to focus on unsubstantiated discrimination or to lash out at others. Rather than face the truth about herself constructively, she may put up defenses against society.

Unfortunately, a lot of women's magazines and women's organizations encourage this attitude. It is much easier to be an "innocent victim" than a woman truly responsible for her own growth. It is very like the behavior of our own teenagers, who blame their parents for their own emotional turmoil when it is something in themselves that they must accept, learn from, and grow through.

Church law and custom are often cited as barriers to women's full participation as the People of God, and so they are. But in this situation, as well as in others of everyday life, a woman needs to ask herself: "*Who* won't let me, society or my own lack of ingenuity and courage?" A woman needs to look first within, to question and refine her intuition *through logic and an acceptance of the facts,* and *then* take hold of her power to change what sorely needs to be changed. Unless she first confronts herself, a woman may find herself working out her own unresolved problems instead of the very real ones in society.

Another highly emotional and intuitive — but equally futile — response to the felt need for change in our lives lies in **turning all our aggression inward.** The aggressive way of too much "passion" is to blame others; the passive way of too much "patience" is to blame ourselves. It may seem to a woman in mid-life that everything — all the meaninglessness and turmoil and anger — is somehow her fault. "If I were a better person," Ann said, "I would have more patience with the kids, try to understand my husband's moods. If I really loved him, I could make this marriage work again. If I were any kind of Christian at all, I wouldn't *hate* so much." Shocked at our own emotions, we again resort to blame; but this time we direct our anger at the deepest part of ourselves and set into motion the slow black spiral into depression.

This is an acquired feminine response to crisis: most of us learned as little girls that feelings of anger or aggression are bad. So we try hard to pretty things up and let only selected feelings through. It may be all right to feel hurt, but not enraged at the one who hurt us. It may be all right to sigh and resignedly pick up yet another pair of shoes left on the living room floor. But a "good" wife and mother does not admit her own deep bitterness at being taken for granted and hides the self-hate that comes because she can't seem to change the situation.

We do not know what to do with such overwhelming emotions. We try, as it were, to swallow them whole, to make them disappear from our lives. Swallowing this anger, however, is like swallowing poison. It leads to further hurt — sometimes to the physical problems so prevalent in mid-life: lack of energy, gastrointestinal or gynecological symptoms, headaches, backaches, allergies. Unacknowledged anger, anger with no safe outlet, turns like a cornered animal to attack the one who blocks its escape. We are left with a medical problem that is very real, not "just something in my head," with pain and physical damage as real as the anger, bitterness, and frustration that caused it. Doctors have long recognized this fact. Some even see in anger and emotional wounds the ultimate root of *every* illness, and even of most accidents.

There seems to be within the human person some profound honesty that cannot deny the power of what we are feeling inside. If we try to hide our anger, try to cover up our inner wound, it becomes insistent, more and more tangible and "real" until it finally breaks into our consciousness in a way we can no longer deny. The inner wound then becomes visible in our outer physical self. One woman, for example, was attacked by severe asthma several months before her emotional problems otherwise surfaced. These caused her to consider taking her own life, and the method that kept occurring to her — hanging herself — was like the asthma attacks themselves, a physical expression of how she felt deep inside: choked and literally suffocated by the anger she tried to stifle, by emotions that kept her cut off from the breath of new life.

* * * * *

We have seen how the inner energy that gives rise to the great yearnings of mid-life can be, out of fear, terribly misdirected. At this time in her life a woman often feels a great need to share, to give of herself in a passionate outpouring of all that she is. But she must recognize the need, first, to patiently become her true self — to take her own life into herself and to nurture it with a view to giving birth to an entire new self.

All too often this patience sours into depression or martyrdom when it is desperately needed to bear one's own painful weakness, to sort out one's threatening emotions, and to trust in the goodness God has laid within us like a newborn infant. Mid-life, in truth, is meant to be a psychological second spring, a time of unprecedented growth, when women are called to develop the passion and patience which are meant to be put in the caring service of the world.

2

The Other
Half of the Story

We have seen how, to many women approaching mid-life, the whole world seems to be falling apart. We have looked at the situation symptomatically, and it presents a very bleak picture indeed. There seems to be no way to cope with our own choking emotions or with the terrible loss of meaning. When life takes off its benign mask and we face the ugly terror of confusion, personal inadequacy, and depression — with or without divorce — everything we have ever known, our whole world, begins to crack.

Yet, it can be, if we choose it, the first tear in a cocoon we have outgrown, a confining and protective covering that keeps us isolated and in the dark. We have seen that the "crisis" of mid-life is a normal stage that comes upon all adults in one way or another — whether they admit it is happening to them or not — whether they rise to the challenge of it or not. We may be afraid of the word "crisis," and so deny we are facing one; but the elements of *"decision"* left in the term from its Greek origins can heighten our awareness of its promise. At mid-life we are faced with unparalleled opportunity to grow, and we must *decide* what to do with it.

Although at times it feels like we are cracking up, a closer look at what is happening from a psychological point of view shows it is only the cocoon of our outgrown self that is really cracking and crumbling. A similar thing took place in adolescence when the young adult inside outgrew childhood and began to work toward independence. Mid-life is like a second adolescence, rife with confusion and pain, but a period of transformation to greater maturity.

The first half of our lives was spent learning about the outer world and adapting to it, finding out where we fit. We did this, each in our own way, by observing what was around us and judging what we saw. Psychologist Carl Jung spent a great deal of time observing these seeing and responding "functions," which he found to be basically four: sensing, intuiting, thinking, and feeling. We have already seen how our capacities to function in these ways can be misused during mid-life, but now we need to take a closer look at them and how we've used them.

In the first half of our lives some of us tend to gather data by using the senses — how things look, smell, feel, or sound — while others use their intuition, taking in the feel of a total scene all at once.

Once observation has been completed, the two groups also tend to operate in quite different ways in arriving at judgments about what has been perceived. The data-gatherers usually become thinkers and use logic to link ideas and to form conclusions; the intuiters function better on the basis of their feelings and evaluate situations through their emotional response to them.

One way is no better than the other. But by the time we are forty years old, we have gotten used to observing in one way and judging in one way. The other two functions — the other two ways of observing and reacting — have been seldom used, and so remain undeveloped, like seeds in the ground.

And there they stayed, the equivalent of a whole new personality, germinating quietly within us. At mid-life they are ready to spring forth. At mid-life we are ready to begin relating to the world in a whole new way. It is time to grow, to see things differently, to perceive and respond to creation in a far more complete manner. God meant this time to be a gentle unfolding and blossoming of ourselves.

But, as we have seen, there's a hitch. For many of us, the way we function is the *only* way. Human beings seem to be afraid of what they are not used to, of what is in the dark. Many of us, by age forty, have learned to despise our unused capacities. And so, an intuitive wife may look down on her husband "who can only see what's under his nose," while secretly doubting her own ability to handle facts like math or money or the political world. A thinking man may show little patience with his wife "who takes everything *personally*," but may be so afraid of expressing emotion that he estranges his own family.

Yet, all four ways of functioning — sensing, intuiting, thinking, and feeling — belong to the psychological makeup of every human being and are given to us by God to make us more fully alive, to help us love. In spite of our rejection of some of them, all these ways of perceiving and judging are our heritage, a whole second self germinating like the seeds in Jesus' parable, without our even knowing how, and wanting to develop like a baby in the womb. Mid-life is like spring, a time of birth, the time we must at last accept our other self and embrace who we are in our totality.

The second half of life is meant to be quite different from the first. It is a time when we are called to an inner journey, to discover and integrate the whole of ourselves. It is a call to reconciliation with our hidden "other half," so we may evolve into the beautiful and unique individual God created us to become. It is a deeply holy and wonderful call, redolent with Easter imagery — hatching chicks and emerging butterflies and babies being born. But it always hurts to bring forth new life. We women, of all people, know that. And Jesus taught us the spiritual dimension of that truth through the transforming mystery of the Passion and Resurrection.

Mid-life is such a difficult passage because for forty years we have worked hard to define ourselves and to fit in, and now all that is being shattered. The role of wife and mother, so right for so long, now feels like a confining shell, while our emerging self seems vulnerable and weak. We feel called to develop our intellect and independence; and then we discover how afraid we are of the world, of using our own gifts, of exerting our own assertiveness. We feel a new sensuality; yet, we are constrained by a deep mistrust, undeniably derived from our religious traditions, of our body and its sensations.

For the Christian woman who values her religion, her home, and her family, the problem becomes a spiritual dilemma. Women's liberationists taunt us: "Develop yourself and seize independence!" Our religion haunts us: "Empty yourself and gain salvation!" We know we *must* grow, *must* understand and accept the self struggling to be born; yet, not for one instant can we forget our husband and children and those around us. As Christians we know the whole point of coming to love and understand ourselves is to love and understand others. This is the greatest pain of the mid-life passage: we know that we have to do both.

Since women usually go through the mid-life passage first, our husbands do not understand any better than we do what is happening. They may feel threatened by the changes in us, interpreting our restless desire for something more as a rejection of what we already have — a rejection of themselves and all they have worked so hard to achieve.

The situation may be even more complicated if our spouse is confronting *his* particular mid-life challenge at the same time we are. He may suddenly feel called to accept his emotional or intuitive side, to turn his attention to feelings and relationships. Yet, these traits are exactly the opposite of the logic and objectivity men have developed in the competitive world, and may seem to reveal weakness and inadequacy. He may feel threatened by a wife who suddenly seems strong and aggressive, ready to tackle the world. Yet, if they but understand what is happening, the pain of mid-life for both husband and wife can be the pain of birth — the birth of their last child, a new relationship in which their marriage is transformed.

3
Meeting
the Challenge

How does a woman begin pulling herself out of the emotional turmoil in which she is not only engulfed but which seems to fill her very self as well? The only answer is to look at it honestly and confront it directly. She must look within and accept everything she finds there. Her job now is almost like that of the Creator, who looked on chaos and called light and life and all green and growing "good" things out of its darkness.

A woman in mid-life, looking within, will find *anger,* and she can call it good. It is right for a human person to become angry at wasted potential, for anger fuels action for change.

A woman in mid-life will find great *limitations,* and this, too, she can call good. To know I am finite, that I can't save the world, and that not everything depends on me is tremendously freeing. It frees us to trust the drive toward wholeness in our children, the goodness within our spouse, our own instincts, and the loving providence of God.

A woman in mid-life will find *ambition,* a drive to accomplish something in the world, and this she can call very good. She is fully capable of reaching out to the world and using her talents and personal power to nurture what needs caring for in our society — the environment, those discriminated against, the peace of the world, the least of the little ones, each other.

We were *right* to feel everything we had was not enough, because there was more; and this more was *"me,"* my whole and entire self.

Discovering All That We Are

In order to find this true self, in order to attain true maturity and individuality, Carl Jung learned that a woman had to go beyond cultural stereotypes and expectations and discover what a real woman is and can do. She has to acknowledge her own inner capacities for very "masculine" things, her God-given gifts of *thinking* and *sensing* — the powers that mankind has always associated with action, strength, and the outward thrust. These so-called "masculine" ways of functioning have nothing to do with sex, but are part of every woman's psyche, her hidden gifts. In saying this, we are not being reverse chauvinists. Men can integrate themselves as well, by recognizing their own "feminine" capacities and beginning to develop their own gifts of feeling and intuition. Our ideal is embodied in Jesus, an adult who was both assertive and tender, powerful and vulnerable, passionate and patient.

Sensing and thinking, then, will be two ways in which a woman in mid-life can get out of herself and into the world. Beginning to function in these ways will provide her with dual outlets for the release of her own passionate potential. This is so because they will direct her pent-up energies into the reality of physical creation and make her powerful or potent as we are meant to be in the real world. Jung saw this when he called this outgoing side of a woman the *animus,* a very masculine Latin term for "force" or "soul." This "force," once freed, will give her the courage to face what is happening inside her, wrestle with it, and win.

Women sometimes resist the development of these capabilities. Logic and objectivity strike us as cold and heartless. We see how a strict adherence to logic or to the rules or to the corporate structure can demean people and put barriers between them by day — barriers that contemporary society then tries to beat down at night with mindless sex and violence — the sensing function run wild. The shiny chrome coin of technology has its darker side, and we want none of it.

Yet, it is also true that much of what we know about the wonder of creation, about medicine, farming, or the stars, has been learned through loving observation and logical deduction. Objectivity has enabled us to heal each other's hurts, to nourish our families, to be aware of the infinite diversity in the world God made. It is essential to our happiness because it roots us in the real world, where God planted us and means us to be fulfilled.

Cultivating the objective can help us love by removing the projections we have cast on to other people and in seeing them as they are. For these reasons, many women beginning to function more in these ways are surprised at the sense of relief and freedom they experience, as when a breath of spring air sweeps through a closed room. They know women can still trust their intuition and respond with the heart, but that they must exercise their latent functions to bring their perceptions into better focus and to correct them and to enhance immeasurably their reactions.

Moving Beyond Stereotypes

To achieve her own potential, then, **a woman must first recognize her capacity for doing things in a rather "masculine" way and take this into account when she formulates a fuller definition of who she is, a definition that goes beyond outgrown roles.** This will help her face the fact that, at mid-life, her children no longer depend on her in the same way they did before. Little ones needed us in the role of "mother" — a constant presence giving a great deal of physical care. But as they get older our children are going to need our wisdom and maturity, our knowledge of life and growth and the world. It is going to be less and less helpful to relate to them as children who must be cared for (making them "props" for our role as mom) and more and more necessary for their growth and ours that we see them as independent individuals in their own right. We will have to accept them at a far deeper level, as responsible persons, as friends, as unique beings created with their own mystery and destiny in God.

Our role as "mother" is ending. Of course, we will always be, in one sense, a mother; but that is not *all* we are, neither to our children nor to ourselves. We, too, are unique persons, with talents God gave us and with something to accomplish in our world. Mid-life is the time to unearth our inner resources and decide what we want to do with them, time to focus our generative and nurturing energies in a new direction. Whether we are working inside or outside the home, discovering our fuller role will involve reaching out, standing on our own two feet, and realizing that no one is responsible for our lives and happiness but we ourselves.

Developing Our Potential

Once we have redefined ourselves, we can, without embarrassment, begin to **make use of our gifts of observation and logic. Focusing them on our intuitions and feelings** will help us further separate from the chaotic feelings of mid-life. We begin by being completely honest with ourselves and asking ourselves some hard questions: What am I feeling? Why? Where can I go for help in clarifying how I feel? Once we admit we are actually feeling something and can name what we feel, then we can begin working *with* our emotions rather than denying or repressing them.

In mid-life we are often people who feel angry and afraid, resentful and bitter, restless and depressed. But that does not mean we are bad, inferior persons. Many women deny what they feel because they never learned that emotions in and of themselves are neither bad nor good, that they just are. God endowed every human being on the face of the earth with emotions: even Jesus felt anger and fear and exasperation with those who would not hear. Emotions are morally neutral; what we choose to *do* with them is the important thing. Only behavior is right or wrong; feelings never are. This is very hard for many of us to understand, for we were brought up hearing, "You shouldn't feel that way" or, "It's wrong to get mad." It may be wrong to express anger in a violent way that hurts someone else, but feeling anger is normal to human beings and never wrong.

Communicating Honestly

Once we realize that emotions are what make us human, the raw material with which we create ourselves, it is easier to take the next step and **be honest with *others* about how we feel.** It sounds so simple, but for many women it is very hard to say, "When you do that, I feel taken for granted. I feel no one cares about me as a person." Or, "I disagree with you. I think this way about it." Often, we are afraid to express our feelings to others because we think conflict may result.

"I can never tell my husband how I feel," women often say, "because it would make him too angry." There are two assumptions underlying such a remark: first, that I am responsible for my husband's feelings, and second, that he cannot handle his own emotions. Our job in mid-life is not to take on such monumental responsibilities or make such big assumptions about someone else but to be *honest* in a Christian manner.

An excellent way to do this is by giving an "I message" instead of a "you message." Family counselors explain that "I messages" communicate something about ourselves, contain no judgments about anyone else, do not

38

injure relationships, and are very likely to promote a willingness to change. Every "I message" involves five elements:

1. A nonjudgmental **description** of what is happening — "I want to tell you about my day, but I see that you are reading the paper."

2. An **interpretation** of what this means — "Not much communication is going on between us lately."

3. A **statement** of "my" feelings — "I feel lonely, that no one is interested in me, and I want to share things with you."

4. An **expression** of "my" wishes — "I would like you to tell me when you are finished reading so we can talk a little while."

5. A **request** for a response — "Are you willing to do that?"

This is very different from the "you message," which would probably go something like this: "That newspaper again! That's all you ever do anymore, read the newspaper. Can't you take an interest in what goes on around here? Why don't you talk to me?" Here is a lot of talk about "you" and sarcasm that hurts the other, but absolutely nothing about my feelings, what I would like changed in the future, or an invitation to help make things better. Giving an "I message" to my spouse is a way of loving him because I am showing him a very deep part of myself, thereby expressing my trust in him.

Testing Our Intuitions

Telling others how we feel is also a means of testing what our intuition seems to be telling us. Emotions are an automatic response to our perceptions; so, if our perceptions are askew, then the emotional response will often be inappropriate. Asking "Did you mean that in a sarcastic way?" or stating "I feel uncomfortable when you are so quiet because I think you're angry at me. Are you?" are two simple ways of clarifying what seems to be going on between us and our spouse or boss.

At mid-life we make our own the prayer of the blind man at the side of the Jericho road: "Lord, that I may see." The challenge of mid-life is to get our emotions and intuitions out in the open in the bright light of day, to see exactly what they are telling us and if they are appropriate and realistic. Sometimes they are not and need to be changed. Sometimes they are accurate and need to be shared for the good of the relationship.

Conflict may come, but this is not bad. The Christian Family Movement, a nationwide network of families that has over thirty years of experience in dealing with married couples, points out that there *can be no real intimacy in marriage unless there is confrontation.* Spouses must tell one another how they feel, must clarify what they believe their intuition is telling them. This is the *only* way to test our perceptions and, therefore, the only way to change how we feel. Willpower, good intentions, prayer, being nice to one another — none of these work for long.

Testing our perceptions of **ourselves** is important, too. Instead of "just knowing" that we have no hope for a better job or meaningful contributions to make to our community, we should look closely at what we have learned or been doing over the years that could prepare us for a new role. One woman, for example, observed the increase of working wives in her neighborhood and concluded she could market her housecleaning abilities. Another consulted the adult career guidance center at her local college to find out what her skills were and how she could update them to find a job she actually could enjoy. A third is using her ability to be comfortable listening to people by becoming part of her parish's outreach committee that visits the sick and elderly. These women "objectified" themselves enough to see both their strengths and their weaknesses so they could build on the one and counteract the other. Such tasks can never be undertaken if a woman refuses to see herself as she truly is, even if that doesn't seem so terrific at the outset. For a woman in mid-life, "The truth shall set you free" is more than just a pious adage.

Freeing Our Sensuality

Pulling ourselves out of the emotional turmoil also involves becoming truly free in the real world by **using our senses to enjoy and appreciate life. This includes learning to enjoy our own bodies.** Despite TV advertising and playboy stereotyping, sensuality does not come naturally to all women. Many of us have to work at it. Many of us in mid-life suddenly discover we have spent years of our lives with blinders on, intent on doing things for others and trying to please everyone. It was part of the way we were raised. But now it is time to change that, to develop an appreciation of bodily sensations, to find something we enjoy or something we can take pride in just because it pleases us.

Many women have the gut feeling that this is being

selfish or silly, forgetting that the challenge of mid-life lies not only in doing something but also in *becoming* someone — becoming one's complete self, a fully human, fully alive woman. The really selfish thing would be to go through our entire lives too wrapped up in what we "should" be doing or in our own emotions to ever enjoy the physical world God created for us. In his love God has filled our lives with little gifts placed everywhere — the twinkle in a child's eye, the feel of sun on our skin, and, yes, the sensuous delight of a bubble bath! It would be terrible never to see, *feel,* or thank God for them. The way to be grateful is to notice, to enjoy. The whole of creation is available only to those that are really willing to take the time to function as sensitive and sensing beings; for even the deeper realities of symbol and myth and sacrament can only be understood if we experience their outer wrappings. Those who truly appreciate the life and sayings of Jesus are those who have seen the lilies of the field or who have felt soothing oil poured on a wound. Jesus himself knew these things, and Son of God though he was, remained firmly rooted in our real world.

* * * * *

At last we may discover the true use for our hidden tools — the "knife" of our logical discrimination and the "lamp" of our powers of observation. They are not for blaming others or making cutting remarks, not for finding fault and nitpicking, but for interior pruning and the testing of our perceptions, for helping us discern what is true and where to cut away what is false. By using them in a caring way, a woman learns to grow out and up and comes to realize that this maturation is the only way to achieve true freedom. By going out of herself, a woman, paradoxically, finds herself.

4

Discovering Wholeness

We have seen how important is the mature use of our outgoing "masculine" gifts of logic and sensation. They serve to compare our perceptions with those of others and to separate us out of the world. This is a vital step in the process Carl Jung called "individuation," in which we step out of the surrounding matrix and become ourselves.

But becoming an individual is a very lonely job. As we get older, our decisions must come from more and more soul-searching, more and more agonizing over what our real values are; and we sometimes suspect there are no real "right" answers. The danger here is that we avoid the crossroads of crisis, avoid making decisions because the whole direction of life is toward the crossroads. There we must decide and choose, and this choice will lead to yet another crossroad. This is the only path to growth and self-knowledge, to differentiation from the crowd. With our intellect we choose, and so become.

The woman who is afraid of this vital decision-making process will seek safety and approval in the faceless majority. She will dread making waves and crave the security nonassertion brings. The woman who becomes strong enough and sure enough to decide which way to go in life will always leave some group behind. The more decisions she makes, the more people she will leave who are going the other way. She may eventually be walking alone. She realizes that the "knife" of her intellect is meant to be a sculptor's tool, given to her to carve herself out of the block of humanity; and the "lamp" of sensation is the light that shows her how different she is, and how to use her differentness.

We use these tools to form ourselves into unique and beautiful human beings, but at the end of our self-creation we are like Adam and find ourselves alone. The whole creation story in the Bible emphasizes the loneliness of individuation. God even brought all the animals to Adam for him to name, and in this way showed the first human being that he was separate from the rest of creation. The basic isolation we feel in mid-life is a reflection of the fact that all of us are unique individuals, with quite different worlds within us and quite different perspectives on the world outside. We are profoundly alone.

Yet, women in mid-life can bear this fact without panic, indeed with a kind of joy, because saying "I am alone" is also saying "I am unique."

Becoming unique is so important, not because individualization is the end of our development but because true connectedness is. It is not good, God said, for us to be alone, even if this aloneness is the direct result of our growth. It is important to become uniquely myself because only true individuals can relate and form community. No hope of a real relationship exists between people who are so immature that they have never discovered their essential isolation. That is why the vast majority of teen marriages fail, and why the divorce courts are filled with ex-wives who were so concerned with "shoulds" that they were never themselves and ex-husbands who could never establish an identity separate from their work. People who have struggled to become their true selves and have borne the loneliness this always entails are ready to tackle the next step on the way to full humanity — the mature use of their emotions and intuition.

This is going to be a hard job because our Western culture devalues and fears both of these functions. Our ability to sense the whole meaning of a situation without detailed analysis is an ability our society labels "women's intuition." *Women's,* notice, not men's. No self-respecting Western male would be caught dead with "women's intuition," with something he could neither explain nor logically prove with his detailed analysis. And so women also have learned to devalue and misunderstand this human gift, just as men have learned to reject it.

Emotions are equally suspect, due, in part, to our own Christian upbringing. We learned it was bad to get angry, bad even to feel too good. Pleasure, particularly sexual pleasure, was associated very often with immorality, as was the body. Modern society purports to care very little about such "sins" anymore; yet it, too, has a real fear of expressing emotions. The aim of everyone, not only of teenagers, is to play it "cool," to appear detached. We feel awkward and embarrassed when someone bursts into tears, and even some modern women (who are "allowed" to cry in our society) would rather die first. For us, emotions are a sign of weakness because in our society power lies in objectivity.

There is great danger in this kind of thinking and the suppression it fosters. There are few things so dangerous as repressing a natural response to a situation. Our four responses to reality have a way of making trouble for us if we ignore one of them or try to stifle it in ourselves. The human psyche strives for balance, and will bring to our attention its unused capacities in quite negative ways, much like an ignored child. And so, concentration on thinking alone will cause the emotions to make a raucous bid for attention, while relying too much on the senses alone will irritate our intuitive self. This may be why our high-tech society is hagridden by violent crime, outbreaks of war, and epidemics of anxiety and neurosis. We try to repress our emotions and intuition, pretending we are completely self-controlled super-beings living in a predictable world; and so we wind up afraid to walk around in our own cities at night. To a society striving at all costs to be completely in control, emotions are bad. To a society convinced that "real" means "tangible," intuition is dark and dangerous. Yet, it is these very traits which make humankind unique in the universe, which tell us extremely important facts about ourselves and the nature of reality, and which are vital in our evolution toward true community in the Body of Christ.

Emotions and intuition exist in human beings to end our loneliness. Used in conjunction with our thinking and sensing abilities, they can be the royal road out of ourselves — the bridge that can cross over the chasms that separate us or the passage that can tunnel beneath our defenses. They are the only sources of compassion and true connectedness between people and God; and, therefore, they are at the root of all true humanity.

Accepting Our Feelings

How, when emotions seem so uncontrollable and in-tuition so unreliable, can we value these things in our-selves? How can a woman in mid-life begin to make mature use of these powers which seem to come so naturally to her yet, also, seem to be the source of all her problems? What are these capabilities *for*?

First, our emotions tell us more than anything else about who we really are and what we really need. If we accept them as our own and do not try to blame some-one else for them ("You make me so *mad*!"), they will tell us loud and clear when we feel taken advantage of, when we feel hurt, when we feel inadequate, when we need to be touched. It is up to our thinking or conceptual powers to name and communicate these feelings to the appro-priate person — ourselves, another, or God — but not to judge them as good or bad. It is up to our senses to gather data about the outer reality of the situation to see if our emotions are appropriate to the actual words and circumstances which triggered them. Although both of these processes will help us focus more clearly on what we are feeling, there is no guarantee we are going to *like* the person our emotions reveal to us — not at first nor all the time — but at least we will begin to see ourselves as we really are. If we listen to what our feelings tell us, we can finally take down the narrow stereotyped picture of the perfect person we had painted of ourselves and discover behind it the reflection of ourselves in the mir-ror of intuition.

Patty's experience will make this clearer. A former librarian, she was brought up to believe that emotions were, at one and the same time, a symptom of "womanly" weakness and a dangerous power that could unseat the rule of logic if not strictly controlled. She was an intelligent person, but she came to think of her intelligence as somehow incompatible with feelings. So, she turned her feelings off, spending tons of mental energy in the process, until at mid-life her bottled-up emotions became too powerful to ignore. They came pouring out in a flood of tears, self-hate, and bitterness until Patty was forced to acknowledge them.

Patty's feelings told her much about herself she did not want to hear: that she had not developed the drawing talent that had emerged even when she was small; that she thought that everyone should agree with her; that she expected too much from herself and others. But her feelings also told her things that, for Patty, bordered on the miraculous: that she was a compassionate person that could actually feel the hurt of others; that she still yearned to express herself by painting (even though her intellect and senses judged she would never get rich doing it); and — to her surprise and great joy — that she truly longed for a deeper relationship with God. Patty was never aware of these strong emotions within herself because she never allowed herself to *feel.* Emotions to her were something to repress in fear and shame, her weak and seemingly helpless self. Perhaps it was the undying spark of intuitive vision that enabled Patty to glimpse, even at the very beginning of her struggle at age thirty-eight, that she was good, that the emotions she feared were, as Jung said, "ninety percent pure gold."

When we look honestly at who our emotions tell us we are, we see at last how right our basic intuition was: I am not enough. The self we know, the self we have allowed to develop so far, *is* not enough. But we can laugh and shout for joy at this, for there is more to us, a lot more, a whole new self waiting to be acknowledged and embraced. When we accept what we have too long suppressed, it is very much like what happened to Saint Francis of Assisi when he kissed the leper. He looked and saw the face of Jesus. When Patty accepted the fact that she was a sensitive and very emotional person, she was free at last to see the great goodness hidden within her.

Becoming Sensitive to Ourselves and Others

Still more promise lies in those sensitive powers of emotion and intuition. They can be used to bridge the gap between persons. If we can learn to accept and embrace our true self in all its dimensions, then we can more easily learn to accept and bear with each other.

In meeting the mid-life challenge, we have learned a lot about pain and healing, about our own weaknesses and our own possibilities. We have grown singularly equipped for compassion, which means "suffering with" another. We know now how it hurts to become fully human persons. We have become more aware of what we feel; and we know we must bear with ourselves in patience, no matter how petty or shrewish we appear to ourselves. This kind of self-acceptance is the beginning of acceptance of others.

Not only were we right when we felt "I am not enough" but we were also right when we felt "My husband and children aren't enough." No spouse or child or parent or lover *is* enough for any human being. I am not enough for my husband either; both of us as human beings need more understanding and love than we can ever give each other: we need the unbounded love of our Creator who made our hearts for himself.

My husband is not enough, and therefore he is just like me. He, too, experiences the terrible and glorious struggle in which everything is crumbling and another self is being born. He, too, plods from day to day, stifled by humdrum details which make everything seem like nothing. He may be less articulate, have less awareness of what his feelings are, but the hurt is the same for him, too. He also longs for acceptance, desperately needs patience, and is full of passionate potential. We *know* how he feels. Even the dim realization that they and their spouses are going through the same thing spurs many women to go for help. They no longer want to lash out in blind hurt. They want to withdraw their projections and to see both their spouses and themselves as they truly are.

Carl Jung bemoaned the fact that there are no colleges for forty-year-olds that would teach them what they need to know about life's second half. Even if there are no schools to enlighten us, there are counselors, psychologists, or pastoral ministers that can help. Once we have glimpsed the goodness God put into us, we realize that going for help is no luxury but often the only way to unlock the inner potential of *both ourselves and others.* In the close network of family relationships, we may be the knot which prevents the untangling of all the other knots. Family healing has to start with someone, and most often it is with the wife because her acute mid-life struggle has made her so aware of her weakness that she has had to either reach out to others or despair. Eventually, our spouse may become willing to accompany us, but even if he does not we can learn through counseling how to make the most of the pain we have experienced and to grow in patience and compassion with ourselves and others.

One of the first things we learn will be how to listen — really listen, with no defensive answer ready — to those closest to us. This is risky in the extreme, for we know by now that words hurt. Yet, gradually, as we learn how to express our own needs and emotions, we can afford to let our spouse express what he really feels, without our crumpling instantly into tears or getting out the big guns. The more we refuse to defend ourselves by attacking the other, the more we listen for feelings, the more we will see that our husband often feels just as afraid, confused, trapped, or angry as we do. Through the use of "I messages," we will begin to see that his expressions of emotion, even that of anger, are not really attacks on us but statements about himself, about how he feels. It may take counseling and a lot of time and patience; but, finally, in that beautiful phrase we find in the Gospels, we will be "moved with compassion" and begin, at last, the long journey out of ourselves to the other.

When we try to open ourselves to others in this way, we are being like Jesus. This is the way he healed and the way *we* are healed. When Jesus touched and healed others they saw their own goodness. They responded to Jesus with love and faith, which evoked even more compassion in the Lord and gave him the strength to continue his mission as Savior. Love always does that; it is like helping the other take off a heavy winter jacket — and then feeling the summer sun on *our* arms. When we open to someone and love them, it is like rain and sun penetrating to the seed under the hard ground in each of us, and both lover and beloved unfold and grow together.

If we learn compassion, then not only will the present look different to us but so will the past. In mid-life our own children teach us we have very painful limitations and are not perfect parents. We don't always know what to do about our teenagers, how to reach them, how to equip them to deal with the world. If we work to accept this weakness in ourselves with patience, then *we can begin to accept the weakness of our parents and forgive, at last, the mistakes they made in raising us.*

Patty, for example, for a long time had resented the rigid and unemotional way her father treated her as a child. But a closer look at the past made Patty realize that her father grew up in the shadow of his own mother's serious depression. This dark emotional atmosphere in his boyhood home eventually sent one brother to a mental institution, but Patty's father was one of the few in the neighborhood who eventually graduated from high school. He learned to rely on his objective powers of thinking and logic to combat the unexpressed and, therefore, terribly frightening emotions all around him. "My dad survived," Patty said. "He passed down to me the only survival techniques he knew. I can see now that I owe my love of knowledge for its own sake to him." This was a great gift, even though the other side of the coin that Patty received was a rigid denial of emotions and intuition. Yet, this entire coin, rightly saved and spent, acquired for Patty a far deeper understanding of both her father and herself.

Becoming reconciled with the past is a great step forward, and often it becomes possible for the first time only in mid-life. Then we are able to approach previous hurts with enough patient objectivity to *see* and enough passionate concern to forgive — to realize that for- giveness is not even necessary, only understanding is.

Staying Aware of the Personal

A third way of using our inner-oriented gifts of emotion and intuition is much needed today, and that is in making allowance for the personal. A great deal of evil is done in our world by "the rules" — patterns of handling "things" dictated by institutions like corporations, governments, churches, unions, bureaus. These, and not individuals, seem responsible for the huge evils of poverty, hunger, racial and sexual discrimination, and the gross devaluation of human life. All institutions say they are acting for the good of the majority; yet, somehow a great many people get hurt in the process of "business as usual." One wife and mother may seem to be able to do little in the face of so insurmountable a problem, but nothing will be done at all if her "masculine" powers are turned aggressively against others instead of being used to wake up and guide the heart.

A strange thing occurs when human beings see and do not look away. The problems we confront at first seem monstrous and overwhelming — but only if we look at the victims the way society does, as one faceless mass. But the more we get the facts and look, the more individual faces emerge and the more we *feel* with and for them.

Some of the faces we see belong to people very close to us, and we can listen to them or visit them or do whatever small thing compassion suggests. We may even see our own faces as part of the problem, we who are selling our souls to the corporation we work for or "raising" our life-styles to include more and more consumption or voting without regard for Christian values.

We may see, with a shock, that for years hungry people have been lining up at a soup kitchen only ten minutes away from our door. Suddenly, our church bulletin or community newspaper may seem full of invitations to us, full of the call of needy people, full of concrete and practical ways we can help right now. Any woman who uses her eyes to engage her heart will find a way to bring the compassion of God to others and will herself be a force against structural sin. "But I'm only one person!" is the truth indeed, but that is our power and our glory as well as our weakness. Only "one person," only the one who has become an individual in her own right, will have the passion to care, the strength to suffer with the burdens of another, and the patience to trust in God.

Opening Up to the Mysterious

A woman in mid-life can come to value her "feminine" traits for a fourth reason: for their power to open her up to the mystery inherent in human life. Our gifts of thinking and sensing are beautiful, but they stop at the surface appearance of things — right where our society is content to stay. But human beings need far more than logic and sensation, and that is why so much of our society suffers from the terrible sense that beneath all the glitter and the chrome there is nothing at all. Intuition is the ability to find *meaning,* to sense the mystery. Meaning will always emerge in the small and near, in something easily overlooked. Big things like wars or even weddings overwhelm us; what is happening comes home only in immediate details — a sprawled body, the bright joy-filled glance of a groom for his bride. The *"patient functions"* — our emotion and intuition — teach us to value the present moment as something indescribably precious; they free us from the frustrations of the past and striving for the future. These things hardly exist, as far as love is concerned.

Intuitively, then, we will always value things our society sees as weak or irrelevant, especially symbols, myths, and dreams. These things proceed from the realm of the unconscious and give life to our conscious selves; yet, we generally misunderstand them and do not take the trouble to learn about them, thus cutting ourselves off from deep wells of meaning.

Society trivializes symbols into superstitions like hex signs or a rabbit's foot because it fails to see in created objects the embodiment, the incarnation, of a reality too deep for words. Anything God made, if approached with enough respect and awe, holds enough meaning to become precious to us — a burning candle, a leaf, bread and wine. The Eucharist can only be understood in this way, with "patience," for only intuition and emotion can take us far enough to grasp the reality that eludes sense and logic. If we see truly enough, and very much with the heart, then the world is full of God.

Another path to this deeper reality lies through myth. Even though our society usually translates this word as "an untrue and fanciful tale," suitable only for children or the credulous, our very history is shaped by these great theme-stories. We read in the newspapers about troubled persons violently acting out their own inner fantasies or about political leaders who try to play the role of gods. The themes of the struggle against evil, of the journey into peril, or of the wounded healer are perpetuated in our motion pictures and fantasy trilogies just as surely as they were passed down by storytellers throughout the history of humankind. We hunger for these things; so, epics like the *Star Wars* series draw record crowds, while the characters of fairy tales and myths have invaded the language of psychology. We need to make these great mythological themes our own, to become conscious of how they can surface in our own lives.

One woman, for example, came to see her own situation in mid-life reflected in a fairy tale that has been told for generations. The story of Beauty and the Beast told her in symbolic terms exactly how she needed to treat her own emerging other half — the sympathy and gentleness required — if it were to emerge as the helpful inner partner she needed for true happiness.

For thousands of years human beings have told other kinds of intuitive stories — those of the god who came down to earth, of a savior who died and rose again. Jesus lived out this myth, and the stories he told and that we tell about him have a way of mirroring our lives at a very deep level.

Patty had heard all her life the Gospel about Jesus curing the paralyzed man at the pool of Bethsaida, but it never meant much to her. One Sunday, however, when she was thirty-eight, it suddenly spoke to her heart. "I stood there in church and heard the story as if for the first time," Patty said. "It struck me how much I was like that poor man at the pool. He had been paralyzed for thirty-eight years and could never reach the water and be healed, just as for thirty-eight years I could never reach an acceptance of my own emotional nature. I was crippled, too, rigidly denying my very self. But all at once it was as if Jesus stood above me, looking at me with his eyes full of compassion, asking 'Do you want to be well?' It was as if the Lord held out his hand to me, and I took it and felt his loving touch."

Patty was not cured as fast as the man of Bethsaida. It took her a long time to get used to the water. But her encounter with Jesus was as real as the paralyzed man's and the first step on the way to wholeness. Looking intuitively at the Gospel story, Patty saw her own situation and responded with joy to the healing presence of God in her.

Another way to listen to our intuitive selves, to be open to the healing that wells up from God's Spirit within us, is to change our attitude toward dreams. For thousands of years dreams were taken seriously, as they are in Scripture, as a way of God speaking to us; and today psychologists see them as a deeply buried part of ourselves seeking expression and acceptance. The interpretation of dreams has nothing whatever to do with dream books or lucky numbers, as society would have it, but only with ourselves. Most of the time the characters we dream about are aspects of ourselves, and we might learn something from them if we begin by asking: "How am I like this person?"

That knowledge can come from dreams will not surprise us if we remember what dreams are — the unconscious self trying to communicate with the conscious. If we believe God has placed his Spirit deep within us, we will come to see it there, promoting this "unity dialogue" within us. We have only to let ourselves be drawn into it, listen to its wisdom with both mind and heart.

The overall responsiveness by which we know ultimate reality immediately reveals something very deep bearing us up, a nourishing sea on whose warm surface we are carried. A woman who feels its life coursing through her will be at peace and free to act in her world with love because she senses the meaning and goodness beneath all things. She can bring this peace to family or friends when they come to her with the seemingly trivial events of their day. She listens for their feelings, and this very listening often paves the way for insight. Such a woman has learned from her deepest "feminine" nature to let go, let grow, to trust the God present in all things. As troublesome as they are, as humbling as they are, as uncontrollable as they are, intuition and emotions are great gifts desperately needed in our world and in our homes, and we need to be thankful for them in ourselves.

In this process of accepting and developing all of our powers we see an ever-changing blend of passion and patience, of the "masculine" and "feminine," of reaching out and looking within. In mid-life a woman is called to be as courageous as any knight facing inner dragons, yet as accepting as the princess kissing the frog. She must learn to develop her "masculine" traits of sensing and thinking, while always cherishing her "feminine" capacities for emotion and intuition. She learns to look at the behavior of others analytically and yet, at the same time, with compassion. Balancing her own intuitive emotionality with objectivity, she learns to see what is really happening around her and that others are hurting also. In mid-life a woman learns she, too, can take the initiative for change, and that her great need to be needed providentially coincides with all the needs that exist in the world. It all comes together when the two parts of herself mature, meet, and finally embrace in compassion and joy. This process, like marriage, slowly and quietly ripens into the birth of our true self. This process, like nuclear fusion, releases in us a burst of creative energy. And then we see the paradox inherent in our humanity, for patience releases an extravagance of passionate love, which, in turn, rejoices to undergo and wait for all things.

5

Undergoing Conversion

Just as mid-life passage has profound social and psychological implications for women, so also it has profound spiritual implications. It is an opportunity for real conversion, a turning to God with all that we are and can be. At last we are able to love God with our whole heart, our whole soul, our whole mind, and with all our strength.

This is so, to a large extent, due to the suffering this stage of life brings. Mid-life can be a time of conversion precisely *because* it is a time of suffering. Pain always causes us to turn inward. "Why me?" we ask, and thus begins the long search that can lead to our central core. The first fruit of dealing directly with crisis is interiority.

This, remember, also happens to be the whole thrust of the second half of life — a turning inward to compensate for the outer orientation of our first forty years. It is a preparation for the journey into eternity, to the kingdom of God which is both within and among us, both inside and outside our self. Our intuition is already urging us on the long sea voyage, and our thinking and observing powers are being asked to find their security in a critique of direction rather than a vision of goals. This is the point at which the Spirit takes over at the helm and provides safe passage for our deeper selves to where we could not otherwise go.

Once we have journeyed awhile and left behind the earthy, green reality we have always known, we discover that the baggage we have brought along has undergone a sea-change. We have learned a few things, out here all alone under the sky, and discover that head and heart have contributed new insights to old beliefs.

The Cross

The first thing many women discover at mid-life is that a cross is not something up there on the wall but a part of the very life-event they are now facing. They find that mid-life is a crucifixion as well as a crossroads.

It becomes our cross because we are stretched between opposing needs and demands. On the one hand is our passionate urge to accomplish something in the real world, but on the other hand is our longing to patiently attend the mystery we sense within. Painful emotions contradict one another inside us as we struggle to balance what seem to be diametrically opposed ways of reacting. We want to stay married and listen for feelings, to be of service to others, but no one seems to notice our own crying needs. Sometimes it feels as if God has abandoned us, as if he was never really there at all. Our old defenses have been stripped away, and such vulnerability hurts. We see our bleeding emotions and humiliating weaknesses superimposed on our own rigid expectations, and we truly experience what a fourteenth-century mystic called "the painful cross of self."

In this state of crisis, Christians look to the symbol and reality of the crucified Jesus. Father John Welch, in his book *Spiritual Pilgrims,* says that all the darkness and pain we feel is "present and yet transformed in the symbol of the crucified. The shadows have been entered into, not shunned, and the great irreconcilables of life are stretching the figure taut. The human psyche can fully recognize itself in that image." Both Ann and Patty, while going through the darkest days of their mid-life turmoil, turned almost instinctively to the cross. Both of them wore one as a medal over their hearts. "For me," Ann said, "it was a symbol of everything I was going through."

The more we consciously enter into this sign of the cross and the more we understand the pain of what is happening to us, the closer is our bond with the suffering Lord. As Saint Paul said, we learn "how to share in his sufferings by being formed into the pattern of his death" (Philippians 3:10). If we consciously accept the "pattern" of the mid-life passage — the suffering brought upon us by our own inner immaturity and growth and only secondarily by the failings of others — then we finally begin to understand the profound meaning of the cross. We see that Jesus came to share our human hurts, to be one with us when we bear "the painful cross of self." We are with him very intimately when we try to follow him through crisis and see he could bear the agony of the Cross only because he trusted very deeply in his Father.

Jesus endured his Passion with a profound and humble patience.

The inner journey, then, leads not only to our true self but also directly to Jesus. The whole "crucial" experience is a call to conversion that reverberates in this true self, for it is a challenge to give expression, here and now, to our trust in God no matter how much we are hurting. Mid-life is a call to embrace with all our strength the tension of opposites; only through fully experiencing both polarities can we achieve what psychologist Edward C. Whitmont calls "deeper and truer martyrdom," in the original literal sense of the term meaning "witness to the mystery." It was the way Jesus lived and died and rose to triumphant life, the way he showed his open heart to us.

In mid-life we become aware of the cross's relevance to human experience; it is the shadow we cast on the ground when we open our arms to life.

Spirituality

We soon discover that a second bit of baggage that we brought on our trip has changed. At this stage, women discover that religiosity is different from spirituality. Religiosity is rife with "rules." Its symptoms are concern for an unchanging institution, an emphasis on sin, guilt, and man's fallen nature, as well as a conviction that God will love us only if we are good. "Good" is strictly defined by certain behavior, mostly having to do with sexuality. Religiosity is insecure and, therefore, fears and condemns the body and the emotions and avoids intuition as dangerous. Rigid self-control and logic — these are the ideal.

Religiosity reduces faith to a belief in *ideas,* sees human beings as problems, and holds that God is approached through the mind. Spirituality, on the other hand, believes in *someone,* sees human beings as mysteries, and believes God comes to us through the heart. It sees the ordinary person as endowed with immense depth and capable of actually experiencing God. Religiosity plays it safe, declaring that only special people like saints or mystics (usually long dead) could ever have a real relationship with God.

Women at mid-life know better. As wives and mothers, they know, from having looked within, that logic is not the way toward nor has an act of will ever been the true starting point of any true relationship. What *is* the starting point and what continues to fuel the will to faithful commitment is a glimpse — however brief or dim — of the vulnerable heart, of the goodness inherent in the other. It is this intuitive grasp of wonder and our surging emotional response to it at very deep levels which make our will strong in the day-to-day struggle. We have seen the beauty of the other and cannot betray that vision, even when the boredom, loneliness, and pain that are part of every marital relationship threaten to obscure it.

At mid-life it becomes possible to experience the beginnings and growth of this kind of relationship with God. The way, at last, lies open for us to become aware of and open to the possibility of God touching us in ways we can *feel.* We can sense his presence in all of the three common meanings of the word — intuitively, emotionally, and physically. When we accept our "feminine" traits which are, paradoxically, both passionate and patient, the way lies open for us to be "touched" by Jesus. This can happen through a parable, through a scriptural image of Jesus that we can't forget, in a dream that moves us to tears whenever we think of it, or even in a longing desire to feel his presence. It is at these times that the line between body and spirit blurs, and Jesus becomes real to us in ways he never could be before. It is good to stay with these things and listen to them with the heart, for they are the gentle touch of God. Through them we know at last how much he loves us and wants to draw us close to him. All our lives, we knew intellectually that God loves us and dwells among us, but now we "know" this in the biblical sense of experiencing it. This knowing experience of the unconditional love of God is the beginning of true spirituality.

But such an experience of God cannot happen if we insist on its impossibility, if we adhere to a logical religion which enshrines dogma and rejects all the immediacy of feelings and intuition. True spirituality trusts first in God, in his patient care for us and in his passionate love for us, and only secondarily in man's or woman's logic and will.

Sin

The idea of sin is some very heavy baggage that we have hauled around for a long time. Religiosity tends to concentrate on sin, focusing on blame and guilt, instead of on the immense love of God. We learned all too well that human beings were all conceived in sin, and literally beat our breast while murmuring we were sinners "through my fault, through my fault, through my most *grievous* fault."

We were often encouraged to judge ourselves as sinners, while piously being reminded that Scripture forbids us to judge others. At mid-life we know the reason for the scriptural prohibition — no one knows enough about human motivation and human freedom (or the lack of it) to judge if another has sinned. But at mid-life we recognize also that we do not know our own motives that well either. They go down too deep to fathom — reasons beneath reasons why we do what we do. We have looked at our past, the way our parents raised us and the way we unconsciously raise *our* children, and wonder exactly how free human beings are in their actions. We see how we react out of hurt and that "sinful" behavior is often a pitiful cry for help or the symptom of painful mental turmoil. We look at our own actions and know full well they were not a deliberate turning away from a God we didn't really know nor an attempt to hurt someone just for hurting's sake. We have finally become objective enough, with regard to ourselves, to judge that our anger, our bitter words, all the ways that we hurt others were a misdirected response to the hurt we had gone through because of the so-far-irreconcilable warring halves within us.

On the Cross Jesus knew exactly what human pain was; yet, he also realized that what his people had done to him was a projection of the unconscious inner woundedness of all mankind. He chose to bear the pain, seeing his hurt as coming from their hurt, and forgave. His forgiveness did not imply our sinfulness but our basic *goodness.* He "fore-gave" us, gave himself to us *before* we had to prove we were worthy of his trust and love. He knew we were very good because his Father made us. Jesus did not condemn us as sinners because he realized — felt in his own body — how much we hurt.

Rabbi Abraham Heschel said it is not we so much who believe in God but God who believes in *us.* As parents we can understand that. We have seen how growth in our children often involves conflict, ambivalence, anger, and a struggle with selfishness. Yet, we know they are good persons, and we love them. Our parenting teaches us how God fathers and mothers *us.*

So, if "sin" implies guilt, blame, and the rational control and choice of human beings, we wonder in mid-life how common it could be. Perhaps the greatest "sin" is not selfishness or pride or blasphemy but a nearsighted dwelling upon our faults, instead of gazing upon the tender providence and mercy of God. Perhaps the greatest "sin" is our human obsession with perfection. Hitler's insistence on a perfect German race led to the holocaust, and our society's rejection of a less-than-perfect (or perfectly wanted) child has led to abortion. God has already pronounced his creation as good, and is concerned with *growing,* with compassion — not with being perfect. He believes in us deeply, gives himself to us completely, and holds out his hand to help us grow up in him. Who are we to say he is wrong about us and push his hand away? Who are we to intrude our rigid perfectionism into God's tenderly evolving world?

God's Will and Our Freedom

In mid-life many women reevaluate something else they are weighted down with: their idea of "God's will." Many of us used to think of this as a sort of road map God had in mind for our life's journey. In childhood we turned right when we obeyed our parents; at twenty-one we turned right again and married Joe Doaks; and, perhaps at thirty-two, we turned left with our decision about contraception. By thirty-eight or forty, some of us felt we were completely lost or heading resolutely in the wrong direction, away from God. This was, after all, a very logical and "sensible" way to think about our "journey toward heaven." But the crisis of mid-life is bringing other dimensions into our vision: we find ourselves asking what *our* will is as parents for our own children and what this can tell us about the will of God for us. Way down deep do we want our sons and daughters to become doctors, lawyers, or corporate chiefs? Not really. We observe that the best parents want their children to grow and mature, discover what will make them happy, and make their unique contribution to the world. It is the same with our Father and Mother in heaven: "I have come," Jesus said, "that you may have life, and have it to the full." And Saint Irenaeus discovered that God's will for us is that we be fully alive.

A fully alive person is not one who is totally involved in following the rules but, rather, one who rejoices in who she is, neither judging nor rejecting any part of herself. She is open to growth and change because she trusts that God is in charge. These attitudes overflow, inevitably, into how she views the world and other people. The fully alive person is her own unique mixture of thinking and feeling, sensing and knowing. She is a specially configured hollowed-out vessel, meant to hold her Lord in a way no one else can. She, and all the others who are fully alive in God, was created to recognize and deeply love a God unique to *her,* just as he is unique to each created heart.

It is God's will that each of us make visible a facet of our goodness that no one else can reflect, that we become so bound by our unique individuality that we "can't" do anything but be true to ourselves and to him. God's will is that we become as alive as Jesus is, that we trust the Father's goodness and *our* goodness no matter what. In other words, God's will is our freedom.

This leads directly to another concept that begins to shift in mid-life — our idea of freedom. Americans almost always identify freedom with choice, but by age thirty-eight or so we know that makes for much too narrow a definition. If freedom is choice, then a newborn baby is the epitome of freedom; and human beings become less and less free as they *make* choices. And what about the times when life gives us no choice? We did not choose to feel the emptiness and anger of mid-life, just as no one chooses to get cancer or to see a loved one die. What then? Are we any less free because these crises have come upon us? We begin to see, then, that a great deal of our freedom as human beings lies in our ability to choose whether we will accept or reject what happens to us. We begin also to realize that although there are many ways to reject a crisis there is only one way to accept it: by staying with it, bearing it, working it through.

Jesus could have escaped the Cross by denying the tremendous intuitive knowledge granted him at his baptism, by refusing to work out who he was in the desert, by obeying religiosity's rules against healing on the sabbath and against eating with certain people, or by defining Messiahship in a certain way. But, instead, Jesus chose consistently to be true to God's compassion. He accepted every crisis along the way by answering as deeply as he could the question it asked him, by making a decision about what he would do. His free choices gradually narrowed the way he went until at the end of the only road left was the Cross.

This decision-produced funneling is the exact opposite

of "freedom" as we usually think of it. As a result of our choices we become in one way more restricted, more bound. We say "Yes" to one thing thereby saying "No" to thousands of others. But in another way our choices make us more free, free to be ourselves, because they chip away at what is not us.

Freedom, then, does not so much have to do with outside influences (like a domineering spouse or a jail cell) but refers, rather, to the inner attitude with which we respond to what is facing us. At mid-life most women know that they cannot really be "trapped"; they are not so neurotic as to have objections to every solution offered. Rather, a mature woman, who has struggled to balance the masculine and feminine within, will find there is always a way out, and that it is always *through.*

When we choose not to escape, then we choose at last to deal with what faces us. That is why Carl Jung said that a person who is most bound is most free — free to search deeply within for the strength and trust to bear with the cross.

When Jesus was dying, his hands and feet nailed to the wood, he had but one choice left — to accept or not to accept the trustworthiness of God. The great pain and humiliation of crucifixion, the long struggle with feelings of abandonment and failure — these were forces which were crushing his human spirit, as surely as the wine-press and the millstone can crush grapes and wheat. But such forces can transform too, producing bread and wine; and with his last breath and with all his will Jesus chose, gave himself up to what was and into his Father's hands. That is the way of true freedom, and always involves a passion and a patience which are both love and trust. "True freedom," says Jesuit Robert Ochs, "lies not in the *whether,* but in the *how.*"

Suffering

In mid-life our outlook on suffering itself changes. We have already seen how suffering can bring one great good: interiority. It forces one to search for meaning and to search for it in ways beyond rational analysis. Suffering forces us to find a meaning for itself because pointless pain is intolerable for human beings. The suffering of crisis is itself a question, life questioning us. What are you going to make of this pain? What is your answer to depression, mental anguish, divorce, death? These things await our judgment of them, wait for us to speak and declare life meaningless or full of potential good.

Suffering does not stop nor let up until we find the right answer to it. We may first respond by deciding that the painful situation is all our fault, which, of course, will only make everything worse. Or we can blame someone else, and then find that our whole life has to be spent convincing ourselves of this. If our answer to pain is "It happened because I am unworthy of being loved," or "It happened because I was unable to love enough," the pain intensifies. Both these answers drive us further from others and further from God because both of them deny our own goodness.

In mid-life we discover there is no real answer to suffering, if by "answer" we mean logical explanation. But there is a response. It is a response not of our objective faculties, not of logic and judgment, but, rather, of our intuition and emotion. It finds expression in the Cross and the crucifixion. "Christ himself," says theologian F. H. Lepargneur, "has not come to explain human suffering but to dwell in it, to fulfill it and by that to alleviate it, to replace the need for an explanation by his human-divine presence." Jesus removed the isolation suffering brings and replaced it with compassion, or "suffering with." We look at the Cross and see God *with* us. His Cross is planted deep into our earth, a part of our history; on it Jesus bore in his body the same pain that is in our souls. On the Cross he offers us the naked gift of his faithful presence, of love so open and vulnerable we cannot take in the depths of it. "This is my body," he said, "it is for you." We look at him in his patient suffering and passionate giving and know he is in pain because *we* are. In his almost desperate love he wants to be with us, with us in the place where both Jesus and we have been wounded, and where, therefore, no defenses are left to separate us. The "answer" to suffering, then, the response initiated by our profound intuitive vision, is to hasten to Jesus, where wound calls to wound and tenderness draws out tenderness.

Touched by Grace

In our passage to life's second half, we encounter the Cross. We learn in the depths of ourselves what Jesus suffered, and we discover that the pain was too great for him. He died; they took what was left of him down from the Cross and buried it. But now we encounter something else, and it is incredible. Because we have opened in our pain and need to Jesus and, therefore, shared his Cross, we are somehow touched by grace. We look inside and see how much we long for him, or *want* to long for him, and this is he, his drawing of ourselves to him. It is incredible. In spite of every sense and all logic, I know the Lord is risen. He is with me here and now, showing me his wounds that are also mine. I, like Thomas, can touch them in wondering love and know his faithful presence, his drawing tenderness. Because we have learned about the Cross, in mid-life we learn about the Resurrection. It is Jesus with us and in us, attracting our heart to his. In this way we learn about prayer.

We used to think prayer was saying memorized words; but if we were empty, full of mere logic, then so were they. Then we thought prayer was action; but if we were motivated mainly by duty or guilt, then we wound up exhausted instead of energized. Then we heard about meditation and tried to empty our minds of the swarm of details and worries; but if we feared what the swarm was a smoke screen for, then it was all a waste of time.

A Temple

So often, in the first half of life, prayer was such an empty chore. We were so parched and needy, but our prayer brought no rain. Perhaps this was because we were following the dictates of growth and society and concentrating primarily on the outer world. This was very good and necessary, but prayer must move into the inner realm. In the first half of life we learned we were the "temples of God," and this phrase exemplifies how we were taught to relate to God — objectively rather than personally.

A temple or a church is a very "masculine" structure, a work of planning and measuring, a building constructed by a large group of men who use tools and take orders from a boss. The result is a grand edifice, usually in the center of town, where some people go to "practice their religion." Many churches are beautifully and richly decorated, but most are chilly and dim inside. They are almost always empty, except on Sundays, and we have to get dressed up and go there once a week or else commit a sin.

Till now, going to church may have taken care of the obligation we felt of responding to God. What more could God want of us? We gave him this beautiful place to live in and came to worship him in it, just as the rules said. We made the walls thick and high, the door heavy, and kept God separate from the crass, everyday world. We enshrined and isolated him.

Our religion teachers used to tell us God waited for us to visit him, that he had no company except the small sanctuary lamp. To us as children that made sense; not in any *rational* way, of course, because God does not get lonely or need company. But making a visit made sense in an intuitive way, and as children we sometimes made a solemn visit to God in church. However, as time and life went on, the intuitive and emotional voice was drowned out. We went to school, got married, had children, spent money — all good and necessary things — but there was no time (and it *is* a little odd) to visit churches and to listen to "voices."

But God will not be denied, and it was his voice. In mid-life we finally find ourselves slowing down and allowing ourselves to be overtaken by the pursuer. We begin to take seriously our intuitive knowledge and to let ourselves respond to it emotionally. For we are not only Saint Paul's "temple of God" but also Saint Teresa of Avila's "nest of God."

A Nest

A nest is quite different from a temple. It is a work of intuition and emotion, built by a mother bird working alone and by instinct. She has no blueprints and no boss, but "just knows" where each twig goes. Because a nest is easily destroyed by "progress," it is usually built in a quiet, out-of-the-way spot. It is small, not showy, a common and humble thing.

Human beings respond to nests with spontaneous emotion because they are places meant for fragile new life — individually nurtured new life. There are never congregations or committees in a nest, only a family. A nest is open to the light and air, and to the wind and rain as well. It is a roofless vulnerability. Yet, it is also a cheerful, busy place, full of chicks peeping out their hunger in the sure expectation of being satisfied. A nest is, above all, a place of intimate *presence*. The parent birds know new life depends on warmth and closeness, and at night the mother bird spreads her wings over her chicks and warms them with her own body.

Praying is very different depending on whether we perceive ourselves as in a temple with God or in a nest with him. In the logical and sensible temple we are separated from an awesome and mighty God by priest and ritual, by the institutional norms of cult and ceremony. Like workmen, we fall into line without question because we feel too small to understand the big plan. But in a nest of intuition and emotion we are God's hungry chicks, fed with his own body, as individuals, as *me*. The big plan seems to involve grubbing to find what is needed, giving it, and keeping each other warm. The only rules are to give and to receive in an exchange of love.

We build a temple with tools that are not us, with wisdom culled from others and never internalized, and speak to God with someone else's words. But a nest is made with our own being, and we bring to this kind of prayer *our* experiences and *our* emotions. Sometimes we cannot use words at all, and our communication is only an inarticulate cry. Our nest may be a poor and humble thing compared to the sleek lines of learned piety, but God is far happier with authenticity. It is his kind of perfection.

In a temple we stand on ceremony with God, never letting him (or anyone else) see us in anything but our Sunday best. But in a nest we are completely exposed to God, as naked and vulnerable as fledglings. In this kind of prayer God is my warmth and nourishment, not my judge and king. We are dependent on him, abandoned to him, and trust him to do his loving will in us. Dwelling on our faults is a distraction in this prayer because it takes our attention away from God and places it on ourselves. Beating our breasts because we are sinners is like wrapping ourselves in a cloak of anxious worry. It is much better simply to open and let God see us. We do not hide any wound or sore from our gentle healer, for he longs to touch us with his compassion so we may respond to him with even more love.

In a temple God has his place — up front, it's true, but definitely outside of us. He is up *there,* and we are firmly seated in the back pew. We define our relationship to God in rational terms which serve to distance us from him. But nest-prayer is full of imagery, because that is the only way both to evoke and express what we know to be true between God and us. Jesus himself used imagery constantly to communicate God's nearness just because such imagery helps us *feel.* He tried to help us use our sensing function because so often human beings need to feel things in a physical sense before they can feel them in an intuitive sense. Jesus said, for example, that he longed to be with us as a mother bird is with her chicks. He wanted us to imagine the softness of a feathered breast, wanted to evoke in us emotions of tender nestling, because *that was the best way Jesus knew how to describe God's relationship to us.* He did not define dogma or dispense doctrine, but only put forth the simple image of a mother bird. He understands the heart and, therefore, speaks its language of poetry.

Touched by Grace

In the temple, Pharisees and publicans worry about their sinfulness before God, but in the nest we glimpse our own *goodness.* It is important to cherish these glimpses because our awareness of our own goodness is as fragile as a hatchling, as dependent on our acceptance of it as a newborn baby. It seems that the dragons of Revelation are ready to snatch this awareness from us as soon as it is born. Not only have we been taught not to look at our own goodness lest it "make us proud" but have learned, as well, that it would make demands on us that we do not want to hear.

In mid-life we realize there is no place to lay the new-born God in us but on the straw of our own self, in the humble nest that we are. We have to nurture the realization of God's goodness in us and look down at it with love. We do this when we acknowledge that we listened to someone when we were tired or did an honest day's work or were faithful in nurturing life by preparing a meal or that we responded with joy to the smell of rain. We have to let the good in us beguile us like a baby does. It needs to be accepted, smiled at, nourished, and kept warm in our memory.

Just as we are a loving parent to our own children, so do we need to be parent to our new self. Every good act of ours is a sign of God's creative intimacy with us, a child of his love in us that needs to be cherished to full stature.

In mid-life we lay the awareness of the newborn Christ down to rest in us, and it is the beginning of his life, his Incarnation, in us.

People who worship only in temples have to travel to get to God. They are always in search of him. But people who encounter God intuitively and respond to him emotionally realize he is, and always was, intimately near. He comes to us through, not in spite of, who we are and what is happening to us right now. Our God is nothing like the god our intellect has invented. He is incredible — he pleads for us to love him, to open to him, to respond to his faithful cherishing love for us. He wants us to let him love us, to let him enfold us.

It is ludicrous to think that such a God hides himself from us. Everything we know about Jesus, our incarnate God, shows us how available he is to us; the whole *point* of Jesus is to be Emmanuel, God-with-us. The Son of Man on earth was no recluse or hermit, no holier-than-thou who lived on a mountaintop, but a very compassionate human being who made himself available to crowds of people all the time, even when he needed to be alone, even when he was exhausted from healing, even when he was dying. He seemed to search for ways to be intimately present to people — in bread, in wine, in the very breath of his Spirit. He walked on water and through walls to get to those who needed him.

Sometimes God feels so far off because we are hiding from *him.* We can do this by denying our full humanity and rejecting the "feminine" gifts with which God endowed us to respond to him. Turning to the God within is as simple, and as extraordinarily difficult, as becoming fully aware of ourselves.

In sum, then, prayer at mid-life can be a profound experience of God, available to us for the first time because we are more available to God. We are more whole than we have ever been. We have encountered a crisis consciously, and in it discovered the Cross and the compassion of Jesus. To our great joy, we know our God has become one of us, that he is our risen Lord, and that at the center of all reality, at the bottom of all truth, there is a human heart.

* * * * *

The mid-life passage has been likened to a tumultuous storm, a lonely crossroads, a journey to the farthest shore. But it is really a call to totality, and therefore a paradox. We realize that the tension between our apparently conflicting "masculine" and "feminine" selves is really an integrating force, the magnetic drawing to wholeness which is God's most generous and intimate gift. Then we will know in our deepest heart that we are passionately and patiently loved, and will dare to hope to begin to love in the same way.